First published 1995

ISBN 0 7110 2413 8

© Ian Allan Ltd 1995

Designed by Alan C. Butcher

Published by Ian Allan Publishing

an imprint of Ian Allan Ltd,
Terminal House, Station Approach, Shepperton,
Surrey TW17 8AS.
Printed by Ian Allan Printing Ltd Coombelands House, Coombelands Lane, Addlestone,
Surrey KT15 1HY.

On Somerset & Dorset Lines

Robert Robotham

Front cover:
Work-stained Standard Class 5 No 73051 storms over the summit at Masbury with the 'Up Mail' for Bath Green Park and Bristol on 18 August 1962. The 'Up Mail' left Bournemouth at 3.40pm and carried mails from the south coast up to Bristol where connections were made for the Midlands and North. As a result, this train had priority over all other trains.
The late J. P. Mullett/Colour Rail(SD60)

Diagrammatic map
showing opening and
closing dates.

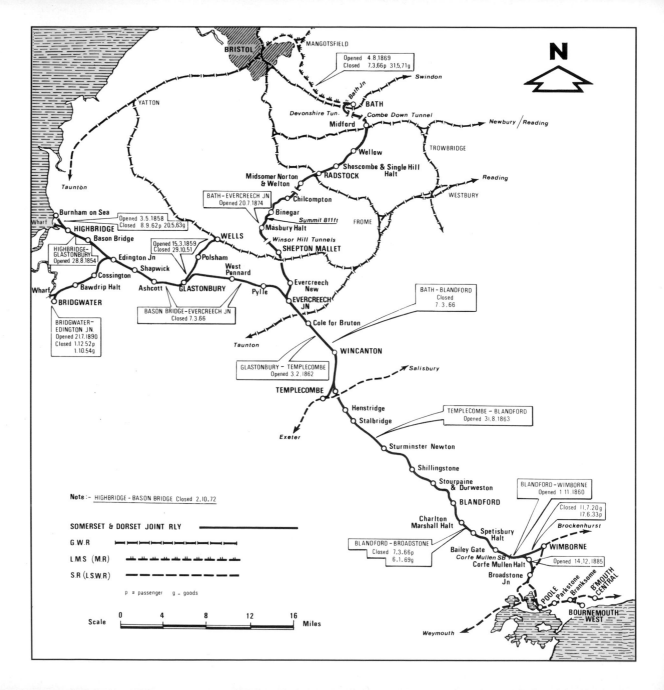

Introduction

The Somerset & Dorset was one of the great casualties of the Beeching era. Like other railways that hold a special interest for me (the Great Central and the Waverley Route), the Somerset & Dorset attracted a large, enthusiastic following which has gone on long after the demolition men moved in. Like on the other two lines, the train crews that operated it were 'special' and drove their trains 'hard' contrasting with those on 'competing' routes. Because of the fierce independence and competition, the 'S&D' (as it was known) seemed like a club, but one that whilst exclusive, was open for the use of all.

The history of the route is well documented elsewhere, notably in Robin Atthill's book *The Somerset and Dorset Railway* and five volumes and videos by that marvellous photographer Ivo Peters. Mac Hawkins' masterpiece *The Somerset and Dorset Then and Now* allows the reader to follow the changes to the route since closure in 1966.

The origins of the line go back to 1854, when a line from Highbridge to Glastonbury was built, opening on 28 August that year. A branch to Burnham-on-Sea was added which opened on 3 May 1858. From Glastonbury the line extended to Wells opening on 15 March 1859. The main sheds were located at Highbridge and the system was known as the Somerset Central Railway.

Further to the south, the Dorset Central started a line from Wimborne to Blandford Forum which opened on 1 November 1860. An extension from Glastonbury to Cole and Templecombe opened on 3 February 1862 which gave access to the London & South Western main line from Waterloo to Exeter. And so the Somerset Central and Dorset Central systems joined on 31 August 1863 to give a through route from Wimborne to Highbridge.

However, the desire for a link through the potentially lucrative North Somerset coalfields, and the passenger opportunities to the North and Midlands proved irresistible and a link to the Midland Railway at Bath (they opened their line from Mangotsfield on 7 May 1870) was opened from Evercreech on 20 July 1874. The whole route was known as the Somerset & Dorset Joint Railway and included an extension from Corfe Mullen to Broadstone and Holes Bay Junction, Poole and Bournemouth, with a spur to the small port of Hamworthy. This link opened on 14 December 1885, after which the link to Wimborne was run down and fell into disuse, a stub only being retained to serve a private siding.

On 1 July 1923 the line was vested jointly between the LMS and the Southern Railway. It was dominated by motive power built to Midland specifications — and was a heavy carrier of freight and passenger traffic — especially during the summer months when trains from a variety of Northern and Midland locations — including Cleethorpes(!) crossed over the Mendip Hills to the holiday town of Bournemouth (together with its Midland Hotel) arriving at Bournemouth West station. Following World War 2 on Nationalisation in 1948, the London Midland Region inherited the role from the LMS of supplying the line's motive power. Depots were grouped under Bristol LMR being coded as Bath, (22C), Templecombe, (22D), and Highbridge, (22E). Radstock was a subshed of Bath, with Bournemouth (Branksome) shed being a subshed of Templecombe by February 1950. From this date, the Southern Region took over from Eastleigh, new codes being Bath, (71G); Templecombe, (71H); and Highbridge, (71J). However, the motive power was considered to be 'on loan', but didn't stop the Southern with the trial of and subsequent introduction of the Bulleid Light Pacifics to the line in 1951. Operations continued virtually unchanged — except for the introduction of the new Standard locomotives to the line — until 1958 when the regional boundary changes put the S&D into the Western Region. All sheds except Branksome were transferred, with Bath, Radstock and Highbridge becoming 82F and Templecombe 82G. This brought a limited amount of Western power to the line, notably pannier tanks and '2251' class tender engines.

The S&D tradionally had its own motive power which was very much 'Midland' in design, most of it being direct builds of Midland locomotives that were absorbed into LMS stock in 1930. These classic locomotives were the '2P' 4-4-0s introduced from 1914 and 1928 which became BR Nos 40323, 40326, 40633, 40634 and 40635; and '4F' 0-6-0 tender locomotives introduced from 1922 and numbering 44557, 44558, 44559, 44560 and 44561 under BR ownership. The famous S&D '3F' 'Bulldogs', BR Nos 43194, 43201, 43204, 43211, 43216, 43218 and 43248, were used on a variety of local passenger and light freight workings, as were the Midland 0-4-4T variants, numbers 58051, 72, 73 and 86, both these classes being Johnson designs. However, perhaps the most famous S&D locomotives were the Class 7F 2-8-0s of 1914 vintage numbering 53800-53810 in BR ownership of which 53808 and 53809 are preserved. These excellent machines were at home equally on passenger or freight work and lasted until the final years of the line. Other Midland/S&D types, notably 0-6-0 '3F' 'Jinty' tanks for banking, colliery and shunting duties (Nos 47310-16), as well as the ubiquitous Stanier 'Black 5' 4-6-0 mixed traffic locomotives, were regular performers.

Interestingly enough, '8Fs' did not become common until the late 1950s. The first tests of the class over the route were done with No 48450 in May 1961 after which they appeared far more regularly on freight turns displacing some of the earlier '7Fs', being based at Green Park (Nos 48436 and 48471). Others were to follow: Nos 48468, 48660 and 48737 in January 1963. The Southern influence on the route brought surprisingly few of their locomotives to work on the line. These were mainly 'Bulleid' Pacifics of all varieties, the most common being Nos 34028, 34039-46, 34048, 34102, 34105 and 34107, being shedded at Branksome in 1959. Class Z 0-8-0T No 30953 was also seen on occasions at Templecombe, being used to shunt S&D trains in and out of the station.

The BR Standard era and the transfer of the route to the Western Region in 1958 did change the motive power scene, but not radically. The Western gradually replaced the traditional S&D types such as the '2Ps' (which had all gone by the end of 1962) and 'Bulldogs', and introduced new Standard Class 4MT, 75000-series, locomotives in greater numbers. Standard '5MT' 73000-series locomotives also transferred in, and some were even painted in BR 'GW' green livery in which they looked very smart indeed. As well as a few GW pannier tanks and '2251' 0-6-0 tender locomotives, smaller Class 2MT 2-6-2Ts of the 41200-series and Standard Class 3MT 2-6-2Ts were drafted in for local services, the '2MTs' and GW '2251s' taking over the Highbridge services virtually in totality.

However, the Standard locomotives that probably had the biggest effect on the S&D were the '9F' 2-10-0 heavy freight locomotives which found themselves working express passenger services. If only these very capable engines had been allowed over the Mendips unassisted (a very rare occurrence), it may have helped cut the costs of providing banking and pilot locomotives that made the Somerset & Dorset so expensive to operate.

They were certainly strong enough — the last 'Pines Express' with No 92220 took 426 tons over the Mendips with the up train (a record unassisted), and the shed master at Branksome had to stop the crew taking another coach to go for the record with the down service! Regular S&D '9F's were Nos 92203, 92204, 92205, 92206 in 1960; Nos 92000, 92001, 92206, 92212 in 1961; and Nos 92001, 92210, 92033, 92245 in 1962. The '9Fs' were all sent away at the end of summer 1962 and the express service, but amazingly they returned in 1963 for a few months (Nos 92220 and 92224) due to a motive power shortage and found themselves pulling three-coach local trains — hardly economical at all! The other Standard type to make a mark on the S&D right up to the end of the route was the '4MT' 2-6-4T of which Nos 80013, 80039, 80041, 80043, 80059, 80067, 80081, 80134, 80138, 80146 and 80147 were regular performers.

The S&D operated an extensive passenger service until the withdrawal of the through express trains at the end of the summer season. As well as the famous 'Pines Express' that ran from Manchester to Bournemouth West, other cross-country expresses ran on the route from a variety of northern locations. These long, heavy trains required two locomotives to haul them over the line up the steep gradient from Bath to Masbury Summit and vice versa from Evercreech Junction.

This double-heading provided spectacular sights out on the line and also an interesting array of combinations of power, ranging from the pairing of a 'Jinty' with a '7F', a 'West Country' with a 'Black 5' or a '4F' with a '9F'. Others pairings were common and virtually unpredictable and I hope this book shows some to good effect. Particularly interesting was the line of pilot locomotives that would stand in the centre road at Evercreech Junction on those hot S&D summer days awaiting the tasks ahead. The heavy nature of the work also made for some unpleasantness for footplate crews as trains slogged up the 1 in 50 through Devonshire and Combe Down Tunnels from Bath junction, especially if you were on the train engine and the pilot was 'chucking it out' a bit! S&D fireman and driver Peter Smith's books *Mendips Engineman* and *Somerset & Dorset From the Footplate* allow the reader to share this experience and are well worth a closer examination.

As well as the expresses, a local service ran along the whole route to support the main trains. After the expresses were withdrawn from the end of 1962 the locals were the only passenger services left. Surprisingly, some were still timed to connect with the withdrawn expresses and thus attracted little patronage. However, one important through service that continued was the 3.40pm Bournemouth West-Bristol via Bath 'Up Mail', which in earlier times (pre-1962) had even taken priority over the expresses. As well, school specials for Bryanston School ran to Blandford Forum from Waterloo, and Downside School was served at Chilcompton.

On the Highbridge line, services generally ran a pattern from there to Templecombe. The service from Glastonbury to Wells was withdrawn in 1951 and to Bridgwater in 1954. Running over the flat-lands of the Somerset levels the line passed through some sparsely populated areas. The local service was supplemented by summer holiday specials that went through to Burnham-on-Sea and lasted from the actual closure in October 1951 to September 1962.

The last years of the passenger service gave the impression of rundown, certainly in the final year of 1966. Official closure was 3 January 1966, but at the last minute one of the replacement bus operators pulled out, so the service lingered on until 5/6 March.

Freight services over the route were built around coal, general merchandise and milk. The inevitable pigeon trains also ran — a scene that is now well and truly gone from Britain's railways. Around Radstock were situated the North Somerset coalfields, collieries being at Writhlington, Norton Hill, Middle Pit, Tyning and Ludlows all of which had sidings or tramways connecting to the S&D route. Another colliery existed at Moorewood. Smaller locomotives (mainly the 0-6-0T Midland 'Jintys') were the usual shunt engines (and bankers), but some exceptions did exist such as the two '0F' Sentinel locomotives Nos 47190 and 47191 and the ex-L&Y 'Pug' No 51202 that shunted the sidings at Radstock, being useful for negotiating a low bridge, and the famous 0-6-0ST *Lord Salisbury* which shunted the sidings at Norton Hill Colliery. As well as coal and associated empty workings, milk traffic originated from Bason Bridge Creamery near Highbridge and Bailey Gate south of Blandford. Traffic from these locations went up to London via Templecombe and it was not uncommon to see milk tanks attached to local passenger services. General merchandise traffic was dealt with by pick-up freight services. Most stations had their own small sidings which gradually closed as freight services were run down. By June 1965 just one goods train ran from Bath to Wincanton; all through services and the Radstock coal trains having being transferred to the Western Region routes.

This book covers the latter years of the route from the mid-1950s to the closure in March 1966 and, through a variety of colour photographs, attempts to show the route in what many would say were its finest, almost defiant years, struggling to cope with a management that was less than enthusiastic about its future and concerned with diverting S&D traffic to its more traditional Western Region routes.

The transfer of the S&D from the Southern to the Western region in 1958 was rather like the transfer of the Great Central from the Eastern to the London Midland Region in February 1958. Seen as a route that was not their own and admittedly expensive to operate, the heavy use of cross-country express passenger services that ran over it began to be seriously questioned. Expensive double-heading did not help and development of other lines made the decision to transfer the expresses away to other 'Western' routes all the more inevitable after the summer of 1962. The same has been mentioned above about freight traffic, but the S&D still served large 'local' towns such as Blandford Forum, Wincanton, Templecombe and Radstock and one would have thought that business from these alone would have been enough to justify retention of the route. However, as with other lines in the 1960s, opposition to closure was not listened to by the authorities and in any case it seemed that the motor car and bus were in an unstoppable ascendancy. It is only now that the towns are becoming clogged with traffic (as residents of Bath and Bournemouth will know) and a cheap to operate 'basic railway' of 'sprinter' type trains may have been the saviour of the S&D, at least in parts such as Bournemouth to Blandford, or Bath to Radstock. However, as Mac Hawkins' book shows, so much has now been built on that this option remains highly expensive and unfortunately, unlikely.

Maybe these photographs are the only tangible reminder of a great railway; one that could have lived on, if only in parts, to play a vital role in meeting the area's transport needs.

As always, special thanks are due to those who have been particularly helpful in my research and with administration. These are Ron White, Mac Hawkins and Wendy Chapman.

Robert Robotham
Charlbury 1995

5

Bath Green Park to Evercreech Junction

Title page:
'4F' No 44102 and 'West Country' Pacific No 34043 *Combe Martin* leave Combe Down Tunnel with the down 'Pines Express' in August 1962. An unusal feature of Combe Down Tunnel was that at the Midford end there was a large hollowed out room used to house an engineer's trolley.
Brian Timmins/Colour Rail(SD131)

Above:
BR Standard Class 3MT 2-6-2T No 82044 stands at Bath Green Park with the curious 8.35am Waterloo-Bristol via Bournemouth working. The station now forms the entrance to Sainsbury's supermarket which has been built next to the site. The date is October 1965, less than a year to go before closure.
A. Wild/Colour Rail(SD223)

Left:
In March 1963 Bath Green Park station pilot '2MT' 2-6-2T No 41304 (with tall chimney) is seen in immaculate condition at the terminus. Despite through passenger traffic having been diverted to other routes after 1962, there was still enough work to be done drawing out empty coaching stock for No 41304 to be usefully employed.
A. Wild/Colour Rail(SD222)

Right:
Standard '4MT' No 75072 awaits departure from Bath Green Park with a stopping service for Templecombe in 1962. The Standard '4MTs', some of which were equipped with the high capacity type tender, were transferred into Bath shed in June 1956, Nos 75071, 75072 and 75073 being the first to arrive in January/February 1957.
Colour Rail

Left:
Bath shed is seen with '2P' No 40601, '4Fs' Nos 44558, 44559 and 44561 and '2MT' No 41243 in attendance on a cloudy day in 1959. The '4Fs' are the original Somerset & Dorset locomotives built at Armstrongs in 1922 and were taken into LMS stock in 1930.
The late B. J. Swain/Colour Rail(SD99)

Right:
'7F' 2-8-0 No 53805 comes off Green Park shed in 1958 for the 11am goods service. The gas holders behind the locomotive are part of a works that had a network of sidings connected to the S&D just east of Bath junction where the S&D main line branches off from the Midland line to Bristol.
Colour Rail(SD262)

Standard Class 4MT No 75023 and rebuilt 'West Country' Pacific No 34042 *Dorchester* leave Bath Green Park on the 7.45am Bradford-Bournemouth West in September 1962. After the conclusion of the 1962 summer service all through services over the S&D ceased.
A. Wild/Colour Rail(SD218)

Left:
Standard 5MT No 73049 in rather grubby condition passes Bath junction with a lengthy local service for Bournemouth in 1960. Note the tablet catcher fitted to the locomotive for the collection of the token for the single-line section to Midford. Nos 73019, 73028, 73049, 73050, 73051 and 73053 were based at Green Park in 1959 to provide more modern motive power for the route, and the class were regular performers until the final year of operation. No 73050 is preserved on the Nene Valley Railway at Wansford.
J. D. Mills/Colour Rail

Right:
'7F' 2-8-0 No 53810 makes a fine sight as it storms up the 1 in 50 gradient with coal empties for Radstock in July 1962. The climb from Bath junction is well shown as are the western suburbs of Bath in this shot. The line then passes through the narrow-bore Devonshire Tunnel, which could be very unpleasant when the going was hard and the loco was producing black smoke.
The late Derek Cross/Colour Rail(SD34)

Below:
'7F' 2-8-0 No 53809 storms up to Devonshire Tunnel from Bath junction — unassisted — the 1 in 50 with the 7.35am Nottingham-Bournemouth express in August 1962, the last summer the express ran. Withdrawn in June 1964 No 53809 languished in Woodham Bros scrapyard for over 10 years before preservation.
Colour Rail

Right:
Standard Class 5MT No 73051 emerges from Devonshire Tunnel with a local for Bournemouth in March 1964. There was a gap in tunnels here, before the next, at Combe Down, was reached. Bath City Council purchased the tunnel some time after closure, and sealed up the portals to prevent access.
Colour Rail(SD16)

Standard '4MT' No 75073 approaches Combe Down Tunnel with the 11.40am Bournemouth West-Bath Green Park service on 13 May 1964. This shot gives a good picture of the high ground that the S&D had to negotiate to exit Bath.
M. Mensing

'7F' No 53809 and Standard '5MT' No 73049 pass Midford's small goods yard with the 9.08 (SO) Birmingham-Bournemouth West in September 1962. This train was booked to pass Midford at 12.10 entering the section at 12.02 and leaving at 12.15. This yard once transported quantities of fuller's earth and still had wagons serving it in 1962 for general goods traffic. *W. Potter/ Colour Rail (SD148)*

Left:
'2P' No 40569 and 'West Country' Pacific No 34046 *Braunton* roll over Midford Viaduct with the down 'Pines Express' on 15 July 1961. The pilot blows off, no doubt with a full head of steam for the climb ahead up to Radstock and Masbury Summit.
The late J. P. Mullett/Colour Rail(SD59)

Below left:
Standard Class 4MT No 75023 and un-rebuilt 'West Country' Pacific No 34043 *Combe Martin* roll off Midford Viaduct with the S&D's named train — the 'Pines Express' — from Manchester to Bournemouth in August 1962.
W. Potter/Colour Rail(SD141)

Right:
Unrebuilt 'West Country' Pacific No 34043 *Combe Martin* leaves Midford with a local service for Bournemouth in July 1963. Following the withdrawal of the through expresses the year before, local services (some timed to connect with the withdrawn expresses!) continued to run.
The late Derek Cross/Colour Rail(SD22)

16

Left: '4MT' No 75027 (now preserved) heads through the Midford valley on 2 June 1962 with the 4.20pm Bath-Bournemouth local. Allocated to Templecombe, No 75027 left the S&D at the end of the year for Machynlleth. It was withdrawn at Carnforth in 1968. *The late J. P. Mullett/Colour Rail*

Above: '2P' No 40634 and '9F' No 92204 are seen on the 'Pines Express' near Wellow in June 1962. Wellow station and its village are surrounded by hills, and the tower of the 14th century St Julian's Church can be seen to the right of the train. *The late Derek Cross/Colour Rail(SD26)*

19

Left:
'4MT' No 75071 stands in Radstock North station with Maunsell three-coach set No 394 on a service from Bournemouth to Bath in September 1961. Radstock was once the centre of the Somerset mining industry and was surrounded by pits that generated much coal traffic for both the S&D and the GWR, who also had a station at Radstock South.
J. G. Dewing/Colour Rail(SD123)

Below:
'3F' 'Jinty' 0-6-0 No 47506 comes off Radstock shed to shunt wagons at Writhlington Colliery. The last section of S&D track to stay in place (apart from that in road level crossings) was between Radstock and Writhlington sidings, finally being lifted in early 1976. The date is October 1960.
Colour Rail(SD167)

Class 0F geared Sentinel locomotive, No 47191, built for the Somerset & Dorset in 1929, shunts wagons in Radstock in July 1953. Radstock was a subshed of Bath used mainly for providing bankers for heavy goods trains up to Masbury summit. Also, some sidings under Tyning's bridge (known as Marble Arch) in Radstock had a restricted clearance, hence the '0F' and also an ex-Lancashire & Yorkshire 'Pug', No 51202, being used.

S. C. Townroe/Colour Rail(SD83)

Further on from Radstock was Norton Hill Colliery whose sidings were operated by 0-6-0ST *Lord Salisbury* built by Peckett & Sons of Bristol in 1906. Here, *Lord Salisbury* is assisted by a 'Jinty' in shunting some coal wagons in March 1955.
R. E. Toop/Colour Rail(SD113)

Above:
'4MT' No 75071 is seen passing the signalbox at Midsomer Norton as it rolls to a halt with an up local from Bournemouth to Bath on 15 July 1961. Allocated to Templecombe, No 75071 has been fitted with a Southern Region-style double-chimney.
The late J. P. Mullet/Colour Rail(SD159)

Right:
'4F' No 44557 enters Midsomer Norton with a Bath-Bournemouth local in May 1960. Another train that was undertaking shunting operations stands on the up road and had been recessed there to allow the passenger train to pass.
R. E. Toop/Colour Rail(SD108)

Above:
'4MT' No 75023 and rebuilt 'West Country' Pacific No 34042 *Dorchester* storm through Chilcompton Tunnel cutting with the 'Pines Express' from Manchester to Bournemouth in July 1962. The pilot is 'going well' and is making a fine exhaust!
P. W. Gray/Colour Rail(SD91)

Right:
Standard '4MT' 2-6-0 No 76019 has just passed through Chilcompton Tunnel on the 1.08pm Bournemouth-Bath Green Park local service on 21 July 1962.
P. W. Gray/Colour Rail(SD92)

Below:
'8F' 2-8-0 No 48660 leaves Chilcompton Tunnel behind with the short 11.15am Bath-Templecombe freight service on 17 August 1962. Note the S&D headcode for freight being one lamp on the smokebox and one over the left buffer beam, as you look at the front of the engine. Passenger services were shown with a lamp over the right buffer as you look at the front of the train. When the Western Region took over they tried to standardise the head codes to the BR system — to no avail!
The late J. P. Mullett/Colour Rail(SD170)

Right:
'2P' No 40697 makes a smoky arrival at the smart station of Chilcompton with a Bath-Bournemouth local in 1959. During the demolition of the S&D, Chilcompton station suffered total destruction unlike most other stations at this time.
J. H. Moss/Colour Rail(SD153)

Left:
Standard '5MT' No 73052 pulls away from Chilcompton with a Bath-Bournemouth local. Note the frost-protected water column and smart signalbox. Chilcompton was situated close to Downside School and special trains from London ran via Templecombe at the beginning and end of terms. Freight traffic from New Rock Colliery passed through sidings to the west of the station. The date is August 1964.
R. E. Toop/Colour Rail(SD103)

Above right:
'5MT' No 73049 and '7F' No 53809 pass Moorewood with the 9.08am Birmingham-Bournemouth West on 18 August 1962. The climb to the summit at Masbury was still fierce at this point, hence the double-heading.
The late J. P. Mullett/Colour Rail(SD155)

Right:
'9F' 2-10-0 No 92001 passes the grassed-over sidings at Moorewood with the 10.32am Bournemouth-Manchester service in August 1962. Moorewood box is in the background and closed on 21 June 1965. A very smart Gresley coach leads the rake of 'mixed bag' stock. Moorewood sidings served a colliery that closed in December 1932.
The late J. P. Mullet/Colour Rail(SD68)

Above:
'2P' No 40563 makes a smoky departure from Binegar on 4 March 1961 with a down local. Binegar was just over one-mile before Masbury summit and at one time provided stone, beer and livestock traffic. In the early years of the 20th century, Binegar was the terminus of the two-mile, 3ft gauge, Oakhill Brewery Railway.
P. W. Gray/Colour Rail(SD84)

Right:
In August 1962 '4F' No 44102 pilots 'West Country' No 34043 *Combe Martin* on the southbound 'Pines Express' (headboard on 34043) near Masbury summit on the final stretch of the climb near bridge number 69 which crossed the road to Oakhill.
J. G. Denning/Colour Rail(SD1)

Left:
'4MT' No 75073 and West Country No 34043 *Combe Martin* storm over Masbury summit with the 10.05am Bournemouth-Bradford on 18 August 1962. At 811ft above sea level Masbury summit was the highest point on the S&D.
The late J. P. Mullett/Colour Rail(SD63)

Below:
The '9Fs' were very capable locomotives and could perform creditably even unassisted on the S&D. Pioneer '9F' No 92000 makes a fine spectacle as it storms through Masbury station with the 9.55am Bournemouth West-Leeds in August 1961.
J. G. Dewing/Colour Rail(SD205)

Left:
'West Country' Pacific No 34006 *Bude* and 'Battle of Britain'
Pacific No 34057 *Biggin Hill* approach Winsor Hill Tunnel with
the LCGB 'final' special that ran over the line on the last Saturday,
5 March 1966. The special ran to Templecombe from Waterloo
and then on to Evercreech Junction and Highbridge and back
behind '2MTs' Nos 41307 and 41269. Then Nos 34006 and 34057
ran with the train to Bath and completed the run to the south again
later in the day.
P. Zabek/Colour Rail(SD21)

Above:
Ivatt 2-6-2T '2MT' No 41307 and Standard 2-6-4T '4MT'
No 80138 pass over Bath Road Viaduct, Shepton Mallet, with the
2pm from Templecombe to Bath Green Park on the last Saturday
of operation, 5 March 1966. Locomotives were being worked away
to the north prior to closure, hence the double-heading.
J. Spencer Gilks/Colour Rail(SD246)

'8F' No 48309 (one of two of these locos fitted with steam heating) runs towards Shepton Mallet with an LCGB special, the 'Wessex Downsman' from Bath on 2 May 1965. This was one of many specials running in 1965/1966 as enthusiasts realised that the S&D was doomed.
J. F. Aylard/Colour Rail(SD206)

'2P' No 40634 and Standard '5MT' No 73052 come off Charlton Road Viaduct, Shepton Mallet with the down 'Pines Express' in March 1961. This shot shows the undulating nature of the S&D to good effect. The viaduct consisted of 27 arches, an unusual feature being that every third pier on the down side is buttressed to resist the lateral forces of fast and heavy trains.
P. W. Gray/Colour Rail(SD52)

Right:
'9F' 2-10-0 No 92001 runs past at Shepton Mallet (Charlton Road) with a southbound train in 1962. The S&D was allocated double-chimney '9Fs' and some are now preserved: No 92212 at the Great Central Railway at Loughborough; No 92220 *Evening Star* as part of the National Collection; and No 92203 at Cranmore.
J. G. Dewing/Colour Rail (SD10)

Left:
Standard '4MT' No 80134 leaves Shepton Mallett with a down local for Bournemouth in January 1965. In the background runs the GWR Witham to Yatton branch which crossed over the S&D to the south of Charlton Road station.
The late David Hepburne-Scott/Colour Rail(SD214)

'4F' No 44560 and '7F' No 53806 make a magnificent sight at Evercreech New with the empty
stock of a pigeon special in August 1962. Evercreech New was situated on the western side of
the village and is today a housing estate.
The late J. P. Mullett/Colour Rail(SD77)

Left:
Standard '4MT' No 75027 makes a fine study at Evercreech Junction with a northbound service on 17 August 1962. The centre road for pilot locomotives that were attached for the climb over the Mendips is seen to the front of the locomotive. No 75027 is now preserved.
The late J. P. Mullet/Colour Rail(SD158)

Below:
'7F' No 53809 leads a Standard Class 5MT on the 9.08 (SO) Birmingham - Bournemouth West express into Evercreech Junction in June 1962. The station house is now a private residence and in the background the sidings for traffic to and from the 'branch' to Highbridge and Bridgwater can be seen. This line diverged to the west at Evercreech Junction 'North Box'.
Colour Rail(SD277)

Left: On 30 September 1962 (a Sunday) the LCGB ran the Somerset & Dorset Rail Tour over the route. '7F' No 53808 was in charge of the train from Broadstone junction to Bath, which also traversed the Highbridge branch. Here, No 53808 is seen at Evercreech Junction. *Colour Rail(SD276)*

Above: The last 'Pines Express' ran on 8 September 1962. '9F' No 92220 *Evening Star* was transferred to the line on 8 August 1962 and provided the motive power in both directions. Here, the down train is seen leaving Evercreech Junction with driver Peter Guy and fireman Ronald Hyde at the controls. It was here that someone hung a pine wreath on the smokebox door.
B. J. Harding/Colour Rail(SD197)

Evercreech Junction to Burnham

Left:
Ex-GWR '2251' class 0-6-0 No 2277 enters Evercreech Junction
in September 1962 with a service from Highbridge to
Templecombe. The superb S&D signals add a touch of atmosphere
to complete the scene. All this is just fields today.
J. G. Dewing/Colour Rail(SD136)

Below:
'2MT' No 41242 enters the small station at Pylle. The signalbox
closed in 1929 along with the passing loop. The train was the
9.45am from Highbridge in July 1962. Pylle's location, over a mile
from the village it purported to serve, did nothing to encourage
traffic.
P. W. Gray/Colour Rail(SD194)

Left:
Ex-GWR 0-6-0 No 2219 leaves West Pennard for Highbridge in September 1963. These '2251' class locomotives had replaced the more traditional S&D locomotives, notably the 0-6-0 'Bulldogs'. At this station the journey began across the flatlands of the Somerset levels.
J. G. Dewing/Colour Rail(SD135)

Above right:
Ex-GWR 0-6-0 No 2247 rolls rather steamily into Glastonbury & Street with a short freight from Highbridge which has picked up wagons *en route*. Glastonbury was the junction for the S&D line to Wells which closed to passenger trains in 1951.
Colour Rail

Below right:
'2251' class No 3201 is seen at Ashcott with an up local in April 1964. Ashcott was a very simple station with just a single platform. The station 'facilities' were not on the platform at this location but adjacent to the road. The loading gauge stands sentinel over a long-lifted siding!
The late David Hepburne-Scott/Colour Rail(SD137)

49

Below:
After Ashcott came Shapwick and Edington Junction where the Bridgwater branch diverged. The route to Highbridge passed alongside Bason Bridge milk factory. Milk traffic was sent to London from here via Templecombe. Here, '4F' No 44272 stands by the River Brue with the tank wagons on 18 May 1963.
R. E. Toop/Colour Rail(SD107)

Right:
'2MT' No 41242 stands at Highbridge (East) with a Templecombe train in August 1963. Highbridge East had five platform faces and was situated adjacent to the GWR Taunton to Bristol line. Following closure of Burnham-on-Sea to passenger traffic (with the exception of summer excursion trains) in October 1951, Highbridge was the end of the line.
R. Tibbits/Colour Rail(SD245)

Left: A view taken from inside Highbridge shed sees '2MT' No 41307 standing by the water tower on 27 January 1966, the year the S&D system was to close. Highbridge was the original headquarters of the Somerset Central Railway whose locomotive repair shops were situated to the east of the station.
J. R. Betley/Colour Rail

Below: Ex-GWR 0-6-0 No 2204 returns to Highbridge from Burnham-on-Sea and is about to cross the GWR main line (just seen on the extreme right) over a flat crossing. The level crossing allowed road access to the GWR goods yard. The allotments look very productive! The date is July 1962.
R. E. Toop/Colour Rail(SD111)

Ex-Midland Railway '3F' No 43427 stands at Burnham-on-Sea on arrival from Highbridge in August 1959. The view looks towards the slipway which descended on to a pier on the River Parrett. The station closed on 29 October 1951 but holiday trains continued until 8 September 1962. *R. E. Toop/Colour Rail(SD 109)*

Evercreech Junction to Bournemouth West

'7F' No 53804 in immaculate condition waits to get under way from Evercreech Junction with a southbound SLS special in 1962. The track layout here reflected the original nature of the line with the 'branch' to Highbridge having easy access, whist trains from Bath had a 25mph speed restriction. *Colour Rail(SD275)*

Above:
'9F' No 92233 passes through Cole (for Bruton) on 18 August 1962 with the 7.45am Bradford-Bournemouth service. Ivo Peters, the great Somerset & Dorset photographer, is seen photographing the train from the signal post.
The late J. P. Mullett/Colour Rail(SD70)

Right:
Ivo Peters exchanges greetings with the train crew as '2MT' No 41242 arrives at Cole with the 4.05pm from Templecombe on 18 August 1962. The signalbox, seen at the southern end of the up platform, was built in an LSWR style.
The late J. P. Mullett/Colour Rail

'4MT' No 75009 and '7F' No 53810 are seen at Shepton Montague with the 7am Cleethorpes-Sidmouth service in August 1962. Here the lines diverged slightly to run under bridge 127. This long-distance train was really two different services using the same stock that waited in Birmingham for a long period of time. *The late J. P. Mullett/Colour Rail(SD157)*

Below:

'9F' 2-10-0 No 92220 *Evening Star* on the 3.40pm Bournemouth West-Bath Green Park (the 'Up Mail') is seen near Wincanton in August 1962. The LMS coaching stock consists of Stanier-designed vehicles, the first three marshalled as a set.
J. G. Dewing/Colour Rail(SD2)

Right:

Standard Class 5 No 73068 approaches Wincanton with the 1.10pm Bath Green Park to Templecombe on Whit Monday, 18 May 1964. This locomotive was not allocated to any of the sheds that served the S&D, and had probably been hijacked by Bath Green Park; a not unusual occurrence during holiday weekends if motive power was below strength.
M. Mensing

Above:
Ex-GWR 0-6-0 No 2277 waits at Wincanton with a Highbridge-Templecombe local service in August 1962. Wincanton station had staggered platforms and in 1933 additional sidings were put in for Cow & Gate and used to dispatch milk for London via Templecombe.

T. J. Edington/Colour Rail(SD202)

Right:
'2MT' No 41242 arrives at Templecombe and is seen passing Number 3 junction with a rather lengthy local from Highbridge in June 1962. A classic S&D signal provides a frame to the scene. No 3 junction was the diverging point for access to the engine shed and lower yard.

J. G. Dewing/Colour Rail(SD126)

Left:
'9F' No 92245 arrives at Templecombe No 2 junction with the 7.45am (SO) Bradford to Bournemouth West. Impatiently blowing off, No 92245 awaits the road into Templecombe Upper station where the connection with the Waterloo to Exeter main line is made. Another locomotive will then draw the train backwards to No 2 junction from where it will proceed on to Bournemouth. The date is August 1962.
J. G. Dewing/Colour Rail(SD128)

Below:
Ex-GWR '2251' class No 2204 passes Templecombe No 2 box and will turn into the main station to make the main line connection. A '2MT' waits in the background to draw the train back from the station. It looks to be a lovely S&D summer's day in August 1962.
Colour Rail(SD279)

Rebuilt 'West Country' Pacific No 34046 *Braunton* passes No 2 box at Templecombe, taking the single line on towards Templecombe Lower and Bournemouth with the southbound "Pines Express" in 1962. The lower lines lead to the engine shed and lower yard.

J. G. Dewing/Colour Rail(SD4)

Left:
Standard '3MT' No 82002 is drawn back to Templecombe Station from Templecombe No 2 with a Bath local in August 1962. The road down to Templecombe Lower and Bournemouth can be seen just to the left of the locomotive.
A. Sainty/Colour Rail(SD125)

Above:
'2P' No 40569 is drawn back down to the S&D route from Templecombe main line station with a Bournemouth train in March 1961. Trains wishing to call at the LSWR's Templecombe from the S&D had to be shunted around the curve and then drawn back by another locomotive or vice versa!
Colour Rail(SD251)

65

Left:
A good view of Templecombe shed with Templecombe No 2 box in the distance is seen in March 1961. Locomotives in evidence are Nos 44417, 43436, 43474, 73052 and Stanier 2-6-2Ts 40171and 40126, in company with numerous wagons of locomotive coal. The brick building was the goods shed, with the engine shed seen behind.
Colour Rail(SD267)

Right:
'2MT' No 41208 passes through Templecombe Lower's snow-laden platform with a local for Bournemouth West in March 1965. The train is about to pass under the LSWR main line from Waterloo to Exeter.

Left:
Standard Class 4MT No 75072 enters Henstridge with a Bournemouth-Bath service in November 1965. Henstridge was situated on the single-track section from Templecombe No 2 to Stalbridge, where there was a passing loop.
Bill Chapman/Colour Rail(SD160)

Above:
'4MT' No 75065 gets under way from Shillingstone with a train for Templecombe in December 1965. One of the passengers seems to have noticed the camera! By this date the goods yard had been lifted.
J. B. Snell/Colour Rail(SD189)

Right:
Standard Class 5MT No 73001 is seen near Stourpaine with a service for Bournemouth of mixed livery stock in December 1965. The locomotive has lost its front numberplate and has one stencilled on the smokebox door with white paint.
J. B. Snell/Colour Rail(SD184)

'9F' No 92220 *Evening Star* arrives at Blandford Forum with the 3.40pm 'Up Mail' from Bournemouth West on 17 August 1963. Blandford Forum was one of the largest stations on the system and is now a housing estate.
Colour Rail

Left:
Standard '4MT' tank No 80067 stands in Blandford Forum station with a special for Bryanston School in April 1965. The Standard tanks were common sights on the route in its later years. No 80067 was allocated to Templecombe at this time, moving to Bristol the following month.
C. L. Caddy/Colour Rail(SD64)

Right:
'7F' No 53809 shunts milk tankers at Bailey Gate in March 1964. This milk was sent up to London in milk trains initially via the link to Wimborne, but more usually via Templecombe or Bournemouth.
No 53809 is now preserved.
Colour Rail(SD264)

Left:
Standard Class 5MT No 73049 looks superb in its green livery as it waits with a local service for Templecombe at Bailey Gate on 26 March 1964. A good load of parcels is ready waiting to be loaded on to the train. The Unigate Dairy can be seen above the locomotive and station building.
Colour Rail

Above:
'5MT' No 73001, without its smokebox numberplate, approaches Corfe Mullen with a service to Bath in August 1965. At Corfe Mullen was a junction for Wimborne, which was the original Dorset Central route, the S&D trains reversing at Wimborne for Bournemouth until the new line to Broadstone was built in *c*1884. A mile of the old route survived to serve a private siding.
The late David Hepburne-Scott/Colour Rail(SD118)

'7F' No 53808 passes through Broadstone junction with an express for the north in August 1959. No 53808 is also preserved like its sister No 53809. Broadstone was the junction for Wimborne and also the cut-off route to Hamworthy and Wareham.
Colour Rail(SD263)

'4MT' No 75027 and rebuilt Bulleid Pacific No 34039 *Boscastle* arrive in Poole with the 10.55 (SO) Manchester - Bournemouth West on 1 July 1961. Sleepers are piled on the platform and it looks as though relaying has taken place. Both locomotives are now preserved, No 75027 at the Bluebell Railway and No 34039 at the Great Central Railway at Loughborough. *Colour Rail*

Left:
'2P' No 40634 waits to leave Poole with a local to Evercreech Junction in July 1961. The '2P' class locomotives were introduced from 1914 for the S&D and lasted into the early 1960s when they were gradually replaced by the newer Standard class designs.
Colour Rail(SD252)

Right:
Another '2P', No 40563, runs across Poole Harbour with a local service for Templecombe, this time in April 1962. No 40563 was withdrawn the following month, with the last S&D example, No 40700, going in September.
Colour Rail(SD250)

Left:
'Black 5' No 44856 passes Branksome loco with the 3.40pm Bournemouth West to Bristol 'Up Mail' in June 1962. Branksome provided crews and locomotives for S&D services and closed on 1 January 1963.
A. Wild/Colour Rail(SD214)

Back cover:
'2P' 4-4-0 No 40563 and spotless 'West Country' Pacific No 34047 *Callington* are seen on the Manchester-Bournemouth 'Pines Express' leaving Chilcompton Tunnel in July 1961.
P. W. Gray /Colour Rail(SD48)

Right:
'2MT' tank No 41214 stands at Bournemouth West with the 5.30pm local for Templecombe on 12 September 1964. Nothing remains of the station today, although the approach roads are now EMU sidings. Bournemouth West was 71.5 miles from Bath Green Park and survived as the S&D's terminus until 2 August 1965 when services were diverted to Bournemouth Central, although some, rather inconveniently, terminated at Branksome.
Colour Rail